Apple Watch Series 4

Complete Beginner User

Guide (2019 Edition)

With Illustrations

Table of Contents

Chapter 5: Secret Tips and Hidden Tricks

Conclusion

Bibliography

Introduction

The all-new Apple watch series 4 has not just evolved but has transformed the series. It comes with the largest display ever. It is completely familiar yet appears totally new and definitely sets the standards for what a watch should be. Series 4 means fundamental redesigning and re-engineering of the Apple watch. Beginning with the curved corners of the all-new and larger display to the S4 chip architecture, everything is minutely thought of. Apple watches have always been unique and personal products and now they have become more powerful than ever before.

The defining feature of the Apple watch series 4 must be the display, as it pushes it even higher. Apple faced a challenge to make the display larger without raising the size of the case appreciably or compromising its battery life. The viewing angles and areas have increased with narrow borders by over 30% and the new display technology LTPO is responsible for improving the power efficiency as well. It gets you through the day with just a single charging.

The beautifully curved corners of the watch precisely match with the radius of its case and create an aesthetically pleasing and continuous appearance. This also means that the imagery and the touch screen extend to the farthest corners of the display screen. The whole interface has been redesigned in order to take full advantage of the huge new dimensions of the display. It now provides more information and greater detail. It also has a new Infographic watch face which can accommodate as many as 8 complications. You can see more as a result and do more at a glance.

The digital crown was created to enable an easy way for navigating on the Apple watches without having to obstruct the display in any way. This mechanism has been completely re-engineered with the Apple watch series 4. The haptic feedback provides precise and clicks like the scrolling. The watch is a miracle of miniaturization and already is one of the most intricate systems created by Apple. The digital crown is responsible for adding more capability in a significantly small space. Its entire assembly is 30% smaller and still has 21% more parts.

It comes with an optical heart sensor which has been a part of the Apple watch right from the beginning. It allows you to check the heart rate quickly and can detect if it falls below a certain level for a period of ten minutes when you are inactive, and thereby a lower heart rate is initiated. It can turn out to be a sign of bradycardia and may be serious in case the heart is not pumping sufficient blood which is rich in oxygen to your body.

Apple watch Series 4 is optimized in all ways and is more powerful than ever before and yet thinner than before. It provides a battery life of 18 hours on a single charge. The all-new S4 chip is not just a processor but is a complete system in package or SiP with the whole system fabricated into a single part. The architecture permits the Apple Watch to deliver great capabilities in a small space. As a matter of fact, it is the only product in the world which completely runs on SiP.

The 4th generation CPU is twice as fast as before, and the apps open even more quickly, and the performance is boasted across the whole system. The speakers are 50% louder, larger, and more powerful than ever before. They provide a dramatically larger sound for the Walkie-Talkie and Siri. In addition to that, the microphone has been relocated on the opposite side for reducing the echo and having clearer phone calls.

Chapter 1: The Main Features of Apple watch Series 4

Many people will have an immediate query about the new Apple watch series 4 and that is, what's new in it? Well, the simple answer is its design. Of course, there is a lot to the watch than just its appearance, however, the way it looks is the obvious difference to be appreciated by anyone. The design hasn't changed that drastically so that it feels like some other device than the Apple watch on your wrist. But that is possibly the biggest change to the original.

There are several Apple watch series 3 users out there who will struggle to pinpoint the difference in the series 4 watch. It is partly because the first 3 versions blended a thick black bezel to the deep black elements by using OLED display. If you are familiar with the confines of the prior screen than this new corner to corner display, it will feel like a serious change and even a breakthrough. Although the design is the biggest advancement in series 4, there are features in it that you will not need ever.

Speed

The Apple watch has consistently iterated the later versions with one consistent improvement and that is speed. Series 1 watch addressed performance restrictions and series 2 made its debut at the same time with an extra GPS for an accurate outside fitness tracking and the series 3 brought LTE for staying connected short of the iPhone.

Series 3 or Series 4

In its everyday use, the series 4 watch

doesn't feel anything different than the series 3 version and it is difficult to pinpoint any major difference. But if you look at it you will immediately see a more aesthetically pleasing and polished watch in many ways. Keeping this in mind, Apple offers 2 generations of watches at the moment, series 3 and series 4. They come in 2 size options for LTE and GPS only but the series 4 is also offered in stainless steel. Series 4 is recommended in case you are upgrading the Apple watches. It feels new in several ways compared to series 3. But if you are buying an Apple watch for the first time and looking to save some money, you may opt for a series 3 watch.

Design

People have been using Apple watches since they were first introduced and have continued using the upgrades annually to get the most out of them. There are many perspectives about people willing to upgrade from the original, but it is generally believed that there is value to be had in the upgrades that are available yearly. The deep dive into what has been changed annually has been worth it as it has changed the user experience consistently for the better. The external appearance of Apple watch Series 4 has been altered in two areas. One is the 38X42 mm size which has been altered to 40X44 mm and the original stainless steel is replaced by the gold option.

Display

There are two versions available in the new series 4 watch, and they come with 40mm and 44 mm displays. The smaller version of the watch just has a feeling of a minor because the decrease in the screen size makes the overall casing feel like a miniature. Although the 40 mm version feels a little dainty on the wrists like the 38 mm one, it displays as much content as the 42mm version which is extraordinary.

The 44mm version, however, is the brand-new territory even for Apple watch. The legendary honeycomb app grid is bigger than ever before and makes it simpler to use. There is more screen there for the user so that the apps can display more content and the text has also become easier to read without having crank up the font size. Even the 40mm version was impressive as that large a screen on to such a small device was difficult to achieve. The 44mm provides a whole new experience especially while migrating from the 38mm version.

Once you have used the new series 4 displays, the old ones will feel outdated. It is just like the difference between the iPhone X and an iPhone coming with top and bottom bezels. Apple uses a marketing term called Retina for their high-resolution screens. The corner to corner screen is called Retina, as a catchy term for what was required.

The small change in thickness is less obvious, but it is there. The series 4 is much thinner than the series 2 and series 3 watches, however, it is not as thin as the first Apple watch. At least not yet. Although it is slightly less boxy, and that makes it feel great. The series 4 also has a great rear. You will not see it while wearing the watch of course but it is admirable. The heart rate sensor has also been upgraded and redesigned to appear less technical and is more balanced. The surrounding area to the heart rate is ceramic and not steel or aluminum. This is a clear upgrade on the aluminum models. It helps the radio waves to pass through, however, it also appears just great.

Gold and Apple watches have a history. The original Apple watch had an Edition Collection having actual gold in it and it came with a cost of $10,000 to $17,000. But these editions were retired when series 1 and series 2 came along. Later, Apple introduced gold and rose gold aluminum versions with normal pricing. In fact, series 3 blended gold and rose gold with a single finish that was a color between the two shades. The SS model has always been limited to space black and silver.

Similar to the iPhone XS and iPhone SX Max, the series 3 has one gold stainless steel option. Although many people are not big on the gold option, this one is really nice. It is not yellow, and it is not pink and doesn't come in your face. A very well-restrained gold coloring. Apple developed a new version of the existing Milanese Loop for matching the new gold SS finishing of the series 4 watch. The original gold edition watches had sports bands and came with leather straps. Some celebrities had specific gold link bracelets made for them. However, there hasn't been an option for the gold Milanese available yet.

The band and the color combination have attracted a lot of attention and in a good way. Not by being obnoxious. Many people notice it and use the word "pretty" for describing it. Well, that is new for an Apple watch. When the watch is new many people ask about it, but nowadays the Apple watch can be spotted in many areas. Wearing the 44mm version will again raise a few eyebrows, especially the new gold Milanese Loop.

The gold stainless steel watch currently comes with either a stone sports band or the gold Milanese Loop. But a combination of the classical leather buckle with the gold hardware is highly desired. For day-to-day use, a black sports band with a gold SS series is highly desirable. You need to buy the black sports band separately at the moment. But series 4 is not just about the bigger display and the gold finishing. There are many new external design differences.

The air vent dots and the microphone of the prior models have now been turned into a single microphone dot and has been relocated from left to the right side. Speaker has become much louder and has a large opening on the left. It is basically used for Siri, alerts, and calls but the music and podcasts still need the Bluetooth audio. The water eject tone, which was introduced with series 2, has become deeper with the change in speakers.

There is a side button below Digital Crown which is now flush with the watch side. It is not as clickable as before but is less visible. This side button appears to like being borrowed from iPhone or iPad and therefore is a bit too gadget-like, whereas the digital crown has been borrowed from conventional watches. The side button is utilized for activating the emergency SOS mode, toggling, and for launching the Apple

Pay. It is also the launching dock for the apps, so the watch needs it.

All this has resulted in one backward step, and that is using the side button for the snooze with Nightstand Mode and alarm. It will still work for you in all probability but is not as natural. However, it is a good tradeoff for visual improvement.

The old red dot has been replaced by the Digital Crown and has a subtle red ring on the LTE models. The GPS-only models have a black ring, which is even less noticeable. It comes with haptic feedback for the first time, which is turned on by default and can be disabled for having the previous experience. The haptic feedback is definitely interesting while flicking through the album art in the apps showcasing music and podcasts or other lists such as the Siri watch face. In this case, every card flip is mapped to the crown click. The digital crown haptic feedback is particularly good for controlling the volume. It provides more precise control. The haptic feedback on other areas seems like being mapped to every tick mark on digital crown and not to the content of the watch screen.

The Watch Faces

The series 4 version comes with a corner to corner display which not only looks natural but accommodates new watch faces by taking advantage of the large canvas. The new faces mean new complications to some of the existing options. Therefore, these options have not been made available by Apple yet. The issue will get faded with future updates hopefully.

Infograph

Infograph is one watch face that is thick with information and can show up to 8 complications in the analog clock. The 4 central complications fit in the circles bigger than the complications on additional faces. The complication on the top center can also show the text in their tick marks in the clock. It is also possible to use a novel favorites complication for showing favorite contacts of the phone app or iPhone. It is a kind of a regression to a friend circle and is plotted to the side button of the original software of the Apple watch.

The other novel center complications made available on the Infograph face include air quality index, moon, earth, solar system, wind speed, and UV index. The four outer complications spots bring in a new complications style which makes use of a gauge for showing info such as low, high and current temperature, the progress of the timer and so on. The complication style is a clever method for showing more info in tight spaces and by still being legible.

The new corner complications options from Apple include UV and air quality index, newer data points on the Weather app of watchOS 5. It is easy to get lost on the customization options offered by the Infograph face and it is a good problem to have as more apps are updating to work with the new watch face. There is a task manager called Things on the top center complication, therefore, the next task will appear in the text around the dial and the circle complication could be the progress ring. You can add things such as humidity gauge to the corner applications. These complications are used to launch applications by a lot of the users but not to see the information so this limitation in variety can be overcome by fitting the app icons on the center slots. This is applicable to the new watch face as well.

Using the task manager Things situated on the top center, complication is particularly nice as the next task appears in the text around the dial, and the circle complication will be the progress ring. Carrot Weather can be used with all its snark turned off in order to add the humidity gauge to one of the watch's corners complications. Many users are just looking to launch the apps from the complications and not visualize the information. Therefore, a single fix for the limitation in variety can be fitting the app icons on the center slots. This may apply to your next watch face as well.

Infograph Modular

The Infograph Modular is the new watch face introduced in the Apple watch Series 4. It features a digital watch for time, an optional position for day and date, 4 circular complications and a large slot which allows the apps to display almost anything. Just below the large slot, there are 3 circular complications and there is one above it. The Infograph Modular is the new watch face, however, earlier the popular one was Activity Digital. The Activity Digital shows not only hours but minutes and seconds. The Infograph Modular cannot do that yet. However, otherwise, it is a better watch face with the capability of tracking the activity progress of the day.

You can see the high, low, and current temperatures in a single slot, the Activity rings in the other and views the updating chart of the progress in activities with numbers on the exact same face which shows the date. And it also launches the Workout app and shows the task progress with Things.

Full Screen

The Infograph and the Infograph Modular are the watch faces that are completely unique to the Apple watch, but many watch faces have different versions that are exclusive to the series 4 watch. Liquid Metal, Fire and Water, and Vapor are the new additions to watchOS5 in the circular mode, however, only the series 4 has a more advanced full screen option. This allows the elements to move around the corners of your display and tick mark each hour of your analog clock.

Kaleidoscope is available and comes with a full-screen option. Color achieves full screen and circular mode with the watchOS5.1 available in beta currently. These modes available in full screen look fabulous on the corner to corner display. However, they take out the alternative to use any complications. The full-screen faces available are visually appealing but are totally opposite to the information-dense faces.

Legacy Faces

It will be inaccurate to call all other watch faces as inheritance, however, that's what most of them feel like on the new watch, especially on the 44mm size variant. Many are updated and have rounded complications whereas earlier the text was vertical. Others take off the background label in a subtle manner and some slots of complications have remained unchanged. The Siri watch face has become larger and is nice for reading at a single glance. Almost all other watch faces feel as if they were designed similar to the Infograph and Infograph Modular in case they were to be created today.

Some of the watch faces feel as if they were made for the series 4 watch and could fit into the category of a full screen. These are Timelapse and Photos. Earlier these faces used to disclose thick bezel around the boxy watch face for older watches. Now they actually shine. The photos are used as a watch face normally in the wild, and that makes the series 4 more enjoyable.

The Invisible Features

There is so much about the display of the Apple watch Series 4 that other major changes will tend to be overlooked. At least yet. Accelerometer and gyroscope both have been upgraded and it improves the activity tracking, however, in a way which fixes the things that were broken. The series 3 watch was already pretty good at this.

Fall Detection

The series 4 upgrade has powered the new addition of fall detection, though. The feature intelligently detects if someone wearing the watch falls and presents an option of calling the emergency services or disregards the alert and automatically tells the emergency contact in case you haven't responded within a minute of detecting the fall. The fall detection is turned off by default when you are under 65. This is because the younger persons many times get involved in activities that can be mistaken as a fall such as playing sports; however, you may turn it on manually.

The fall detection capabilities, along with

the automatic alerting of emergency services, are appealing even to people of younger ages. The supposed faltering during the morning jog or being trimmed by a vehicle in a hit-and-run can be a real worry. Apple clearly warns that all falls cannot be detected; however, this feature has the capability to save lives.

ECG

The novel ECG app on the series 4 watch will present the capability to take electrocardiogram in the upcoming software updates, but the feature is still not available at the launch. The feature makes use of the watch's upgraded heart rate sensor along with the Digital Crown for assistance.

Similar to the fall detection utility, the uses of keeping an ECG reader which is built-in are not obvious in the day-to-day lives for several of the users. However, the Apple

Watch series 4 with its new ECG app can deliver useful well-being information for the customers who otherwise remain unaware of the vital health data.

Update: The all new uneven heart rate uncovering features and the new ECG app is now accessible in the US for users that are 22 years old and older. This app is simple to use and is also capable of sharing the results with the doctors by using this Health app from your iPhone.

Chapter 2: Setting up and begin using Apple Watch Series 4

Well, you have a brand original Apple watch Series 4. Here is everything you must know for setting it up and get moving. Apple watch is one of the most popular devices for time tracking, fitness, and messages on the move and more. But what is great about it is that it looks great as well on all the wrist sizes and it doesn't matter whether you are an 8-year-old or a senior citizen who is 78-years-old. In case you have picked up the Apple watch for the first time, here are the instructions for setting it up and customizing it to your needs.

What's in the box?

The box containing Apple watch Series 4

includes the watch casing which could be SS or aluminum, straps, a magnetic and inductive charger, an introductory pamphlet, and an AC power adapter. The higher end watches of series 4 come with great packaging however, they do not have any additional features. The Hermes watches come with an additional orange sports band.

Setting up the watch and pairing it with the iPhone

The iPhone and the Apple watch may be two different pieces of hardware; however, Apple watch cannot exist without the other. If you purchase a new Apple watch, just turning it on is only the first step and the next one is pairing it with the iPhone. For pairing the watch with the iPhone, you will need to utilize the Apple watch app for your iOS. It comes pre-installed on the iPhone or you can get it from the App Store in case it is removed previously. There are some methods for pairing the Apple watch to the iPhone depending on what marks the best sense for your needs.

1. Automatically pairing the new Apple Watch Series 4:

a. You can launch the Watch app from the iPhone. Bring the Apple watch near the iPhone to have an interface like the Air pods pairing screen that will launch the Watch app. Now, tap the Start Pairing.

b. Move the iPhone close to the watch until the watch is lined up at the center of the yellow rectangle. You will be aware when you have successfully completed the step with a message, "Your Apple watch is paired."

c. Select the option whether to set up the Apple Watch from scratch or to restore it from a backup.

2. Manually pairing the Apple Watch with the iPhone:

In case you cannot get the Apple watch to begin the pairing process automatically there is the option to do it manually. Rather than using the nifty QR-code-style procedure you can use the Apple watch name for starting the pairing process.

a. Launch the Watch app from the iPhone. You can also bring the watch near the iPhone for having a similar interface to that of Air pods paring screen. This will launch the iPhone's watch app. Tap on Start Pairing.

b. Tap on Pair Apple Watch Manually.

c. On the Apple, Watch tap for viewing the device name.

d. From the iPhone choose the Apple watch on the list.

e. Select whether to set up the Apple watch

from scratch or the option to restore the Apple watch from backup.

Pairing the existing Apple Watch with a new iPhone:

Unlike the iPhone, it is not possible to manually take the back up of your Apple watch to iCloud. All the backups are naturally tied to the iPhone Cloud or iTunes backup. Although the watch will keep on syncing its data to the iPhone consistently when you are connected to the Bluetooth or Wi-Fi, it is not possible to select a backup for all your information unless you can manually unpair the Apple watch, which will automatically sync the latest data with the iPhone backup. Now, the question is, what to do when you are switching the iPhone models? Unpair the Apple watch from the older smartphones, disable the Activation Lock, and take backup for the iPhone. Here is how.

Setting up or restoring the Apple Watch from backup:

When you have paired the Apple watch to the iPhone, it is time to set it up from scratch or use the existing backup.

1. Setting up the Apple watch from Scratch: It does not matter whether this is your first Apple watch, or you just do not wish to carry over the older data, it is quite simple to set up the smart watch from scratch.

a. After completing the pairing process tap on Set Up as New Apple Watch.

b. Tap on either Left or Right to ask the Apple watch about the wrist on which you plan to wear it.

c. Tap on Agree to view the OS terms and

conditions.

d. Tap on Agree to confirm.

e. Set up the Activation Lock and Find My Phone both by entering the Apple id.

f. Tap on OK to declare that you understand the Shared Setting for the iPhone and Apple watch.

g. Tap on Create a Passcode for creating a passcode for the Apple watch. Tap on Add a Long Password for adding a passcode which is longer than 4 digits. Tap on Don't Add Passcode in case you would rather not have a passcode for the Apple Watch.

h. On the Apple watch tap on creating a four-digit passcode.

i. Enter your passcode once more to confirm.

j. Set up the Apple Pay (You can set it up later). You might be required to enter the card security code or your entire number depending on the card you are adding.

k. On the iPhone tap on Continue for indicating that you understand the Emergency SOS.

l. Tap on Install All for installing all the accessible watchOS apps on the iPhone. The watchOS apps are added with the iOS apps. Tap on Choose Later in case you do not wish to install all the watchOS apps available on the iPhone.

Permit the Apple watch to sync with the iPhone. When its syncing is finished the Apple watch, it will be ready to roll.

Restoring the Apple Watch from Backup

a. After your pairing process is complete, tap on the Restore from Backup button.

b. Select the concerned backup.

c. Accept their terms and conditions.

d. Set up the Activation Lock and the Find My iPhone with entering the Apple id.

e. Tap on OK to show that you understand the Shared Settings of the iPhone and Apple watch.

f. Tap on Create a Passcode for creating a passcode for the Apple watch. Tap on Add a Long Passcode for adding a passcode longer than 4 digits. Tap on Don't Add Passcode in case you prefer that there is no passcode on the Apple watch.

g. On the Apple watch tap to create a four-digit passcode.

h. Enter your passcode one more time to confirm.

i. In case you are carrying a series 4 version having LTE service and you have not set it up yet or have concealed your plan, you might get prompted to the Set up Cellular for the Apple watch.

j. On the iPhone, tap on Continue for indicating that you understand the Emergency SOS.

k. Set up the Apple Pay or you may set it up later. You might be needed to enter the card security code or an entire number possibly depending on the card you are adding.

l. Now the Apple watch will start to restore from the backup.

As you are waiting for the Apple watch to restore the data, you may view the basic navigation tips on the Apple watch Basics.

Getting more out of your Apple Watch Series 4

When your watch is paired, you may start using it, but there are plenty of options available for customizing the watch. The Watch app is not just used for setting up.

After all, it is not a simple way of managing the Apple watch apps, features, and settings. There is some management also possible on the series 4 itself, but it is relatively easier to tap around the phone rather than using the tiny watch screen for fiddling about. What you select to do next is left up to you.

In case you have many Apple watches or several iPhone models, here is how to use them in tandem with one another. Although Apple designed the Apple watch to be utilized with a single iPhone at a time, you can work around it to use with multiple iPhones.

Although you can easily connect and switch between many watches and a single iPhone, the same is not applicable for a single Apple watch and several iPhones. It is because the Apple watch relies on the phone for syncing its backup data, among other things. Moving to the newer version of iPhone necessitates the moving of the complete backup as well. Although having said that, it is not impossible to use the Apple watch with several iPhone models as well. But first, confirm with yourself whether you need to switch to another iPhone?

Transferring the Apple Watch to a new iPhone

In case you have bought a new iPhone, here is how to move your Apple watch so that there is no loss of any data. Sometimes after you have purchased the new iPhone XS or XS Max or iPhone XR, you will be wondering what to do with Apple watch. Here is how you can move the current wearable to the new iPhone.

How to prepare the Apple watch to move to the new iPhone

Unlike the iPhone, there is no simple way to

manually take the backup of the Apple series 4 watch to the iCloud. It is because the Apple watch backups are not even backups, as the watch borrows most of the data for the paired iPhone. In any event, all this data is saved to the iPhone's iCloud or the iTunes backup. The Apple watch will constantly sync the health and app data that is gathered from the iPhone and from the iCloud via the phone. This is done via Bluetooth or Wi-Fi; however, it is not possible to select when you should sync the information as it happens in the background. Unless of course, you can manually unpair the Apple watch, which will habitually sync the latest data to the iPhone.

While moving the existing Apple watch to your new iPhone, there are 2 ways of preparing, iCloud, and automatic setup.

Since the introduction of iOS 11.2, Apple has decided to allow you to utilize the Automatic

Setup for moving both the iPhone backup and Apple watch to the new iPhone without having to go through the unpairing and repairing process. However, to ensure that the iPhone and the Apple watch are moved over properly, it is recommended that you make sure the watch is updated. It can be done by using the iCloud Health Sync. Also, take a backup of the existing iPhone before the actual transfer to the new iPhone.

Unpair or Repair

In case you are not having the iOS 11.2 or later on your iPhone, or you are not restoring the new iPhone from the old iPhone backup, the best way of moving your watch is by forcing a backup. This is done by unpairing the watch from the existing iPhone. Let's see how to take backup for the Apple watch.

Manually taking backup of the series 4 Apple watch

As mentioned, there is no Backup button available in the Apple watch app to just sync the watch. This is mainly because there is no need for it. But in case you are upgrading to a new Apple watch or switching your iPhone and wish to ensure that every bit of data is synced, you may do it by unpairing the Apple watch when it is connected to the iPhone. It will trigger one last sync to the iPhone before reverting the Apple watch to the factory defaults.

Switching the Apple watch with the new iPhone

Depending on the method you are using for setting up the new iPhone, you will follow slightly different steps for the setup of your Apple watch.

In the case of Automatic Setup

a. First setup the iPhone automatically by following the instructions.

b. After setting up the iPhone, you will get a prompt, "Do you want to use (name of the Apple watch) with this iPhone?" Press on Continue to go on.

In case you select Unpair/repair

a. Ensure that you have unpaired the watch from the existing iPhone.

b. Setup the new iPhone from iCloud or iTunes backup or you may do it from scratch.

c. When your iPhone completes the setup procedure, open the Apple watch app. You may also bring the watch near the phone in order to bring up a similar interface for the Airpods pairing screen. This, in turn, will launch the watch app.

d. Set up the Apple watch from scratch or by using an existing backup.

Switching the LTE Apple watch account to the new iPhone

In case you have bought an LTE Apple watch, you are likely to get a cellular plan for the Apple watch attached to the iPhone account. The good news is that there is no need to move the plan over when you are moving to the new iPhone. Only follow the steps above and you will be all set. This is because your iPhone's number and plan stay the same even when you switch to the new iPhone with a new sim card in it. In case you are moving to the new carrier with a new iPhone and you need to check with the new carrier for the simplest method to switch it is likely that you will be required to this,

a. Terminate the existing Apple watch plan by calling the current carrier. Remember to not cancel the iPhone plan yet.

b. Follow the instructions provided by the new carrier for setting up the new plan and iPhone for transferring the old number over in case applicable.

c. Set up your Apple watch by following the steps listed above.

d. Add the new cellular account to the Apple watch.

Switching the Apple watch to your new iPhone without backup

In case you are thinking about beginning with the new iPhone from scratch and without a backup, you will have two options. First is when you don't care much about the health data and similar such things, you may start from scratch on both your devices. Of course, in this case, you will lose the downloaded apps along with the health data, and all the GPS routes, saved workouts, heart rate data, and achievements. Second is, when you wish to keep the health data, you may transfer it to a cleanly installed iPhone and Apple watch, but you need to use iCloud and iOS 11 or later. In order to do so, you must have the Health snap switched on in the Settings > iCloud. In case you have plenty of health data, you will need to wait for a while before everything syncs.

Therefore, make sure that you do not erase the old iPhone before it is done. Once all the health info has been synced, follow these steps to set up the Apple watch,

a.   Follow   the   above-mentioned unpair/repair instructions for unpairing your watch

b. When you are finished setting up the iPhone, open the watch app. You may bring the Apple watch near the iPhone to bring an interface similar to the Airpods pairing screen. This will launch the Watch app.

c. Follow the instructions to set up and pair the Apple watch with the iPhone.

Troubleshooting tips while moving the Apple watch

If you are having trouble moving the Apple watch over from one device to another here are some suggestions,

1. Problem 1: I cannot pair the Apple watch to the new iPhone: In this case, you will need to disable the Activation Lock on the older iPhone. Verify that the older device is still paired and in the worst-case scenario try to reset the Apple watch from the watch itself.

2. Problem 2: The health data has disappeared: Did you take backup with the iCloud or the encrypted iTunes, or sync the health data with iCloud? If not the data has not been saved to the backup or the iCloud account. Correcting this problem needs you to either create a new backup for the iPhone and the watch and restoring the new iPhone from the backup by utilizing the third-party option such as Health Data importer, or by waiting on iCloud to complete the backup of the health data.

3. Other problems are: Apple has developed a very good troubleshooting page for moving the watch over in case you face any issues.

Chapter 3: Using the Digital Crown on the Series 4

How to use the Digital Crown and the side button?

Here are some subtle Apple watch controls. For such a small device, the Apple watch has a lot to offer with gestures, buttons, and taps. The iPhone X, in some ways, has taken after Apple watch in terms of design. They both have no Home button and are all screen. They both come with a surprising amount of functions despite having a relatively small number of buttons.

Apple watch, like the iPhone X, comes with a side button that can be turned on and off along with a range of other tricks and tasks. The phone also has an interface that is unique to the Apple watch and that the Digital Crown.

Combine the Digital Crown with a multi-touch screen having Force Touch capabilities which are pressure sensitive, and you have a set of tools for controlling the powerful little computer on the wrist. Force Touch, by the way, is an early cousin of 3D touch from iPhone.

The Side Button

It is the only conventional button on the Apple watch. It not only tunes and powers the watch but controls its Dock and emergency features.

1. Pressing and holding the power on and off: In case the Apple watch is turned off, you may press and hold the side button for powering the smartwatch. When the watch is on, you may press and hold the side button for accessing the power screen then Power OFF the slider to turn off the watch.

2. Press and hold for disabling the power reserve mode: When the watch power level drops below a certain mark it goes automatically into a power reserve mode. This mode displays the time and you cannot restore your watch to its full functions unless you connect it to the charger again. Having said that, watchOS also offers a preemptive power reserve mode that can be used if you know that the watch can be used a little later, but you don't wish to turn it off totally. In case you place the watch in a power saver mode manually, you will be able to restore it to its full functions by just pressing and holding the available side button.

3. Pressing and holding for accessing the Medical ID or SOS: The Medical ID and SOS features of the Apple watch are hidden behind your power screen and they can be accessed by pressing and holding the side button. You can swipe between SOS and Medical ID to activate either of the features. Remember, swiping the SOS will put through a call to the local authorities and so it is to be used only in case of emergency.

4. Press only once to open the Dock: The frequently used apps can be stored in the Dock by watchOS. You can access it from any of the interfaces by pressing the side button just once. In order to return to the previous screen, just press the side button one more time.

5. Press twice for activating Apple Pay: In case you are using Apple Pay, you may use Apple watch for paying almost anywhere with the help of a tap-to-pay terminal. It doesn't matter whether you have the iPhone along while doing it. The Apple watch uses skin contact and the watch gets unlocked to authorize the purchase. Only double press the side button for bringing up the Apple Pay interface. Now tap the watch to the terminal.

The Digital Crown

It is probably the most noticeable of the Apple watch's interaction options. It is a physical dial which can be used to spin and scroll or press once and hold to activate various features.

1. Scroll to wake up the watch: In case you do not wish to raise your wrist, just press down the Digital Crown briefly to wake up the watch display. For a subtler revealing, you may scroll up the digital crown to brighten the display slowly, waking it up from sleep. It is a fantastic way of looking at the time or notifications while you are in the dark space or do not wish to bother other companions.

2. Scroll for Time Travel: In case most of your watch faces are active, scrolling up and down the digital crown will activate the watchOS's Time Travel feature. It allows you travel forward virtually or travel back in time for viewing upcoming appointments, how long it will take for the electric car to charge, how much you exercised, and all kinds of complicating options.

3. Astronomy: There is the astronomy face and the Time Travel moves the shadow on the earth and the cloud as it is passing around the sun even showing city lights at the time of night. The location of the globe on your Astronomy face is based on the current time zone. Switch to another view in Astronomy and the Digital Crown will use various time periods. You can tap the Moon, and the Time Travel will spin according to days to show the various phases of the moon at various times of the month. First Quarter, New Moon, Waxing Crescent, Full Moon, Waxing Gibbous, Last Quarter, Waning Crescent, and Waning Gibbous.

You can select the solar system, and you can move day by day or quicker if you spin the crown more rapidly along with other planets as you watch them complete their circulation around the sun.

Kaleidoscope

On waking up, the watchOS 4 kaleidoscope face is pretty tame. It is when you spin the Digital Crown that you can create the kaleidoscope patterns.

Siri

This watch face called Siri embodies the Time Travel feature of the watchOS to offering cards for upcoming opportunities and suggestions. On the face, you may use the Digital Crown for spinning through the upcoming cards between Recent, All-Day, Tomorrow, and Up Next views.

Solar

By using the Solar face, the Time Travel can move the sun position, thereby taking you between Dawn, Twilight, Day, Night, Solar Noon, Twilight, Sunset, Dusk, and Solar Midnight.

Scroll to View

In case of most apps for scrolling the content of the screen up and down, you may use the Digital Crown. Scrolling in inverted like the touch. You can scroll down for page up and scroll up for page down. Some other interfaces are also available where scrolling the Digital Crown will move the horizontal content similar to the watch picker.

Zooming the Photos app on the apps list

In your Photos app, you may scroll the Digital Crown up and down for zooming in and out on a photo. And in case you have the apps organized in a Grid View, the Digital Crown can be used for scrolling up and down on the app grid.

Scrolling to end the workout lock

On any Apple watch from series 2 onwards, the watchOS will inevitably water-lock the smartwatch if you hit the Lock during your workout. This means that you will not be able to interact with the screen that you have disabled with the Lock. In order to do so just scroll up on the Digital Crown until you have filled the blue bubble on-screen and can hear the watch speaker ping.

Scroll for changing the volume

Whether you are listening to audio via your

iPhone or locally on the watch, you may open the Now Playing function of the watch and make use of the Digital Crown for changing the volume of the track. Only scroll up and down for raising or lowering the music, podcasts, or anything else you may be listening to.

Press for home

The single press of the Digital Crown will bring you either to the currently active watch face (in case you are inside an app or a non-watch face interface) or to the complete app list (in case you are starting on your watch face). In case you are in a Force Touch overlay, the press of the Digital Crown can also bring you back to the prior interface. It is similar to the home button of the iPhone or bottom swipe of iPhone X. Just press the Digital Crown for getting back to where you wish to be.

Switching between the apps by double

pressing

When you double press your Digital Crown in rapid succession, there is a way of skipping the watch face completely and move between the currently active apps and interfaces. In case you have Music open for instance, then go to Weather from the Dock. You may double press the Digital Crown for returning back to your Music app. In case you just have the single app open, the double press will switch you between the app and the watch face.

Pressing and holding for Siri

You can press and then hold the Digital Crown to trigger Siri, which is the watchOS digital voice-driven assistant. Siri can also be brought up by just raising your wrist and saying, "Hey Siri." This is possible only if you have enabled the app via the watch app from the iPhone.

Triple pressing for Accessibility

Once you have enabled the accessibility settings from watchOS, you may triple click the Digital crown for bringing up the Accessibility options for the VoiceOver or Zoom.

Button Combinations

Although the Apple watch series 4 is not an old-fashioned video game unless of course, you are running the appropriate app that is, you may still have some added functions out of it by using various button combinations.

Taking a screenshot

In order to take a screenshot on the watch, you can just press on the Digital Crown with your thumb and then use the remaining part of your thumb to press the side button lightly.

Pause a workout

For pausing a workout, press both the Digital Crown and the side button at the same time. For resuming, press the two buttons together again.

Force Quit

What to do in case you have an unresponsive app on the watch? You may always force quit the app or alternatively force a restart of the entire Apple watch. For force quitting the app, press down the side button until you can see the power screen and then press and hold on to the Digital Crown until you have returned to the watch face. For forcing a restart of the watch, press and hold both the side button and the Digital Crown until the screen has grown dark and the Apple logo has appeared.

Multitouch

Even after using all the Side Button and Digital Crown tricks, you will still be required to use the multi-touch gestures for interaction on the Apple watch screen.

Cup the watch for turning it off

Are you aware that just by lightly cupping, covering, or slapping the display of the Apple watch you can automatically dim the display and mute your calls and notifications? It is a great and easy way to save on the batteries of your Apple watch Series 4, and you also get to feel like a secret agent in the process.

Tap for waking it up, selecting, and more

Anyone who has used multi-touch screens will know the prolific use of tapping in such a device. It is no different for the Apple watch. Just tap to enter the apps, tap to switch the interfaces, tap for selecting the options, tap for playing games, and much more. You can tap for speeding your way through the animations as well. One of the most popular uses for the taps is shortcutting your way in a workout.

Generally, when you start a workout, you will have a 3-second countdown before the workout has started. However, in case you wish to begin immediately, you may tap on the screen when the Ready message has appeared, and it will skip that countdown clock.

Swiping for moving, scrolling, and deleting

One thing which is as common as tapping for a multi-touch device is swiping. On the Apple watch Series 4, you may swipe up or down in lieu with scrolling by using the Digital Crown. Swipe between the various options or swipe sideways or up for deleting the cards. You can also swipe for viewing the Control Center and notifications. For viewing the Control Center, you can swipe from the active watch face of your watch and then access any of the controls or swipe down from the top bezel for viewing the notifications by the Apple watch.

In case you have the apps organized in a grid view, the swiping makes it easier to find the app you wish to launch. You can also swipe between the watch faces. You will have to employ edge to edge swiping for this on the currently active watch face for moving between the other saved watch faces. For deleting, you can swipe sideways. The swipes are used to delete faces in both watch face picker and the Dock. They can also be used to quit the apps you no longer wish to use. From the watch face picker, you will be required to swipe up and then repeat the motion again while in case of the Dock, it is just the sideways swipe.

Dragging to scribble or draw

In many apps and interfaces, it is possible to drag the finger along the screen for moving items, drawing, or using the scribble text interface.

Press down for activating Force

Touch

The Force Touch is possibly the most "famous" secret of your watch interface. Force Touch exists to enable the developers to hide further appropriate options for the apps without having to clutter the screen. The Force Touch can be used by pressing down on your screen in many of the Apple and other third-party apps for bringing up the additional features. Or you may use it in the system for adjusting the settings.

Force Touch for switching between Grid and List views in your app list

When the apps list is open, you may press down on your screen for activating the List or Grid view organizing options.

Force Touch for creating new watch faces

The simplest way of creating and adjusting the watch faces is from the iPhone in the watch app. However, you may also use Force Touch for creating new watch faces on the fly. Just press down on the screen of your current watch face for entering the Edit mode and then swipe, or you may use the Digital Crown for scrolling to the right until you can see the New button.

Chapter 4: Using Siri on Apple Watch Series 4

Turning off and changing the Siri's voice on your Apple watch

Many times, you wish that Siri will be quiet. But in addition to the other fancy features, the new Apple watch Series 4 features a chattier version of Siri. It makes use of your voice for activating and answering queries. However, it does not need a keyboard or a large amount of screen space. And as it is contextually aware, it is capable of handling complex questions and commands. This makes it ideal for devices such as Apple watch, in whose case it works faster many times and more conveniently than compared to other input methods.

Setting up Siri on the Apple watch

The Siri available on your Apple watch is essentially tied to the iPhone. If you have ever turned on the Siri on your iPhone, it will automatically get activated on the Apple watch. In case you need to enable your Siri, however, here is how to do it,

a. Open Settings app on the iPhone.

b. Go to Siri and search Settings.

c. Tap on Press Home for the Siri switch on the iPhone 8 or older or press the side button for the Siri switch available on the iPhone X and later versions to activate Siri for Apple watch and iPhone.

Using Siri on the Apple Watch

There are 2 ways of using Siri. One is via the programmed "Hey Siri" command or the second is by manually pressing and holding onto the Digital Crown. In case you possess a series 34GPS-only Apple watch or earlier, all the Siri queries will be processed with the iPhone or a recalled Wi-Fi network. In case you do not have a strong connection with the iPhone or the Wi-Fi network, the watch will not be able to process the command.

The series 4 GPS + Cellular models of the Apple watch can make use of the connection from the iPhone or Wi-Fi. However, they can directly connect to the LTE as well for processing the Siri queries, thereby making them a lot faster while delivering the results.

Depending on the connection, Siri will take some moments for processing properly. After speaking, Siri might prompt you with a quick, "Hang on," or, "I'll tap you when I'm ready," before it responds. During the time, you may let your arm drop back into your normal position. The Apple watch will tap you on the wrist once Siri has completed processing.

Using the "Hey Siri" on your Apple watch

a. Take the Apple watch close to your face, or if you have the wrist raise inactivated, tap on the watch screen to wake it up.

b. Enter Hey Siri followed by the query.

The Hey Siri gets activated in the first few seconds only when the Apple watch screen is on. In case you are not getting it to work, keep it in mind:

How to activate Siri manually on the Apple watch?

a. Press and hold your Digital Crown.

b. State your query or command Siri.

Changing the Siri voice of your Apple watch

In the Apple watch series 2 or earlier, the watch was always silent while talking with you. You could just see the text in response to your questions. However, from series 4 onwards, the Apple watch versions offer a more verbal Siri. It talks to you in response to the questions you put up. Here is a way of changing the voice of your assistant,

a. Open Settings app on the iPhone.

b. Go to Siri and Search.

c. Tap on Siri's voice.

d. Choose the voice that appeals the most to

you.

Here you might be required to connect to Wi-Fi for downloading the additional voices.

Turning off the Siri voice of your Apple watch

In case you do not like hearing the Siri voice of your Apple watch, you can fix it easily. It is not currently possible to change the volume of Siri's voice, and it is more like an On and Off situation at the moment.

a. Open the Settings app from the Apple watch.

b. Choose General > Siri.

c. Tap on the switch for turning off "Hey Siri."

Using Siri with watch faces

Ever since the watchOS 4 came onto the market, you have been able to create special Siri watch faces. Not only will the face provide you with a customized Siri button straight on the watch face, but it will also intelligently pull down from the photos, calendars, and more. It will provide info such as Passbook passes and upcoming weather for you.

---

[1] Staff. Beginner's guide: How to set up and start using your new Apple Watch. (2018). https://www.imore.com/apple-watch-beginners-guide

Setting up the Siri watch face on the Apple watch having watchOS4

When the watch is fitted with watchOS4, there is a Siri watch face in it. In addition to providing easy access to Siri itself, it offers fast and glance able cards featuring info significant to you.

a. Raise the wrist or tap on the watch's display for activating it.

b. Press firmly on the watch display.

c. Through the series of watch faces swipe left until you have reached the end.

d. Tap the + button.

e. Now, scroll through this list. It is alphabetical.

f. Tap on your Siri watch face.

Triggering Siri Quickly and Reliably

Thanks mainly to the external factors such as room noise and other such factors, Siri is not triggered as reliably as it should every time on the Apple watch. Here are some tips to get Siri to work reliably and not get cut off mid-sentence.

1. Force Siri to listen by having the Digital Crown pressed down: The trick will change your Siri usage completely forever and for the better. Although it is not required, you can continue holding down the Digital Crown while asking your question in order to ensure that Siri has understood the full statement. It is typically helpful in a noisy environment where Siri gets confused and doesn't always discern when you have stopped speaking.

2. Use the screen taps to make the "Hey Siri" toil more dependably: In order to save your battery, your Apple watch just listens to "Hey Siri" when the screen wakes up. Unfortunately, this makes the "Hey Siri" a bit frustrating, especially when you have the screen configured to wake up on wrist raise and do not get the phrase out fast enough. Rather you may reset the process by placing your palm on the screen briefly for turning it off. Then re-raise the wrist or press on display for waking it with "Hey Siri" to follow.

Things Siri can do on the Apple watch

The Apple watch Siri might not be as fully featured as the iPhone Siri; however, the digital assistant can still perform a range of tasks, and it can even chat with its iPhone friend if it ever finds itself at a loss. Here is a quick overview of the things Siri can and cannot do for the Apple watch. The voice-activated digital assistant is a big part of the Apple watch.

The watch-based Siri is as good as the iPhone Siri at turning things on and off. You may ask your watch to enable or disable the Bluetooth or turn on the Airplane mode and also enable/disable the accessibility features such as VoiceOver. Siri will not turn on the Power Reserve mode. Siri is particularly good at knowing what time it is anywhere around the world. You can ask for time in your native place or a city across the world. The voice-based assistant can turn on and off alarms and also set new ones, including the repeat alarms.

You can time your activities, such as a short exercise session or a cooking session. Like the iPhone, it can place calls for you if the recipient of the call is on your contacts list. Siri can also handle calendar events for you. It can pull up the next event and can add reminders to the lists. Image searches are also possible by using Siri on the watch. A hands-free Workout app is available on Siri. You may want to view places in a town or see things on a map; Siri will make it happen for you. The Home Kit commands are also possible by using Siri, whether it is thermostat changes, door unlocking, or lighting.

Chapter 5: Secret Tips and Hidden Tricks

Finding the missing Apple watch by using the Find My iPhone app

It happens sometimes. Has your Apple watch gone missing somewhere? If the watch is still online, you may use the "Find My iPhone" app for tracking it down. Apple watch, for a long time, has had a Find My iPhone button available for quickly summoning a wayward phone back. However, what to do in case the watch itself has gone missing? You either buried it accidentally under a pile of clothes or it has possibly gone off on a Pokémon Go walk around. Here is the easiest way to locate the watch quickly. Remember, in order to locate the Apple watch, you will need iOS 10.3 or later installed along with the Find My iPhone app. The Apple watch needs to power on for this exercise to be of any use. Here are the steps,

a. Open the Find My iPhone or download it if you do not have it installed yet.

b. Sign in using the iCloud account.

c. Tap on your entry for the Apple watch.

d. Now, select Actions. If the watch is still powered on, you may track it on the maps as well as mark it as lost, or erase it, or play some sound.

e. In case you have determined that the watch is within a general vicinity, press the Play Sound button. The lost Apple watch will start to make a repeated ringing sound. In addition to this, your iCloud account will receive an email notification informing you that a sound was played.

f. Once you find the watch, you may dismiss it from your watch face by tapping Dismiss.

Controlling the Apple TV by using the Apple Watch

The Siri remote control that is available with Apple TV has some critics. Fortunately, there is a good way to control the Apple TV by using Apple Watch. First, you need to link the Apple Watch to the Apple TV. Here are the steps for the procedure. However, you need watchOS5 or later on the watch, and the TV must have tvOS 12 installed on it.

Linking the Apple Watch to the Apple TV

Before you begin, ensure that the Apple Watch and the Apple TV are running on the same Wi-Fi. In order to ensure this on Apple TV launch Settings app and then go to Network -> Wi-Fi. Likewise, on the watch launch the Settings and then tap Wi-Fi.

1. Ensure that you are in the same room as

the Apple TV, the Apple TV is on, and you are able to visualize your screen on the TV output.

2. Launch the Remote app from your Apple Watch.

3. Tap on Add Device.

4. On the watch, enter the password which appears on the display of your Apple TV.

This will enable you to see the Remote interface for controlling the TV from the watch screen.

Controlling the Apple TV by using the Apple Watch

1. Swipe left, right, up, and down to go to the Apple TV menu.

2. Tap for selecting the highlighted item.

3. Tap on Menu to get back.

4. Press and hold Menu for returning to the Home screen.

5. Swipe right or left to scrub through the media.

6. You can tap to pause or resume the playback.

You will find that swiping the Apple Watch for navigating the Apple TV menu is a lot easier than using that Siri remote. Another advantage is that you can see what you are doing, even in the dark. The only thing to remember is that as long as the Apple TV is on, you may return to the remote interface on the watch at any time just by launching the Remote app.

Setting up Custom Replies

A lot of people use their Apple watch to send messages, there is a special way to set up custom replies, if you would like to send someone a pre-made message such as "I'll get back to you in 30 minutes"

To set up custom replies go to the Watch app on your iPhone > My Watch > Messages > Default replies. Then scroll to the bottom of the menu and click on "Add reply".

Switching to black and white screen

Sometimes the Apple watch 4's screen can get a little too colorful! This can be a disturbance late at night when you're trying to get some sleep and the blue light is too much for your eyes.

Luckily there is an option in your iPhone Watch app. First click on the My Watch tab, ta General > Accessibility, and turn on the Grayscale toggle.

Challenge a friend to a workout

If you'd like to challenge a friend or family member to a workout of any other challenge for that matter. The apple watch provides activity rings where you and your friends can check on each other's daily progress and compete.

This is not only a great way to motivate each other but also a great accountability tool. When you finish a goal, you can receive awards and the best part is the individuals in your activity ring receive a notification about your progress.

To share an activity all you need to do is:

1) Open the Activity app on your IPhone

2) Click on the sharing tab and tap the '+' icon and type your friends contact information.

3) After you've chosen you friend click send and your buddy will receive an invitation.

Once your friend has accepted the invite you can challenge them, check on the progress and even send motivation messages.

Make Text on Screen Larger

The apple watch being such a tiny device, sometimes, you'd like the text to be larger. Using the watch's accessibility settings, you can change the text.

Go to Settings > Brightness & Text Size and adjust to your specific preference.

Control AirPod Volume

A tip many watch users forget is you can control Airpod volume whilst the sound is playing simplify rotate the Digital crown to raise or lower the volume.

Unlock you Apple Mac

The apple watch can also be used to unlock your mac by themselves. This is how you set it up:

On your mac, click on the Apple icon >

System Preferences > Security and Privacy > Open General tab and check 'Allow your Apple Watch to unlick your Mac'.

Check your ECG (electrocardiogram)

With the series 4, apple have added the ECG app so you can record your heartbeat and rhythm so it can check for irregular rhythm of your heartbeat.

To set up the ECG app

1) Click on Health Data > Heart > Electrocardiogram (ECG) in your health app on your iPhone.

2) Follow the on screen instructions to set the app up.

Once set up you can use the application by:

1) Making sure the Apple watch is fitted well on your wrist. Then open up the ECG app.

2) Once open and you're ready, with

your other hand press the digital crown and wait 30 seconds for the recording to happen.

3) Once recorded you will receive a classification you can note any symptoms. For symptom definitions please consult of a medical professional.

Conclusion

If you have an iPhone, you must possess the Apple watch, and you probably should get a series 4 watch. In case you do not have one yet, do not waste any time in getting one as there is no point in arguing that you do not need one or do not need a wearable computer. This is what people of a certain age say about always being connected to pocket computers such as phones.

Although the Apple watch cannot replace your iPhone, at least not yet, it may save your life in ways that will soon be taken for granted. So, you need to enjoy the fun, and sure it keeps you connected as well. It can motivate you to keep active and, let's face it, you must. And all the while the watch is lying in there waiting to spring into action the moment something is needed.

If you are running or swimming and do not have the phone with you but there is an accident, and you need help, the phone let's say is out of your reach for that moment, rest assured, the Apple watch can make the call for help. In case your heart rate gets too high or slows down or even has an irregular rhythm the Apple watch will alert you and will continue gathering data so that you can check with your doctor later and make sure that he has all the information required to help you. In case you are climbing up the stairs or have gone hiking, and you fall or slip and cannot get back up on your feet, be sure that the Apple watch will call for back up.

If that last part is not particularly important to you, you can get the lower version called series 3 and save some money at around $300. If it is significant as it ought to be, get the Apple watch series 4 which starts at around $399 and $499 for cellular. Yes, it is a bit expensive, especially if you already have a connected machine in your pocket or hands. Or it may be on your desk or on the lap. The watch has a great new design, a terrific edge to edge display, and super new complications. The only things missing are sleep tracking, always on time, and an equivalent of the iPhone upgrade program.

If you have an older Apple watch and you are thinking about upgrading to a new one, first consider whether to go for the LTE option. Also consider what works best for you, older model, the new design, or the new sensors. For people not technically inclined, series 0 or series 1 Apple watches should suffice. In order to get the series 3 or 4, you must really be trying to get the new display, fall detection, and ECG features.

If you do not possess an Apple watch yet, you must get one. Not just because the wearable connected computing has become increasingly capable and as a result, inevitable. It will soon become inevitable and so capable that it can save your life. For that one reason alone get the Apple watch Series 4 for yourself and your dear ones.

Thank you for reading Apple Watch Series 4: A complete beginners user guide with illustrations (2019 edition). It has taken some time to put this book together but with the support of our team we did it. If you've found this book useful please leave a review of the book on its amazon page.

Hugo Tallis

Bibliography

Zac Hall. Review: Apple Watch Series 4 — beautiful design, invisible features. (2018). https://9to5mac.com/2018/12/07/apple-watch-series-4-review-2/

Staff. Beginner's guide: How to set up and start using your new Apple Watch. (2018). https://www.imore.com/apple-watch-beginners-guide

www.ingramcontent.com/pod-product-compliance
Lightning Source LLC
Chambersburg PA
CBHW060947050326
40689CB00012B/2583